HOW TO MAKE CANDLES

A Guide for Learning How to Make Candles for Beginners

Text Copyright © Lightbulb Publishing

All rights reserved. No part of this guide may be reproduced in any form without permission in writing from the publisher except in the case of brief quotations embodied in critical articles or reviews.

Legal & Disclaimer

The information contained in this book and its contents is not designed to replace or take the place of any form of medical or professional advice; and is not meant to replace the need for independent medical, financial, legal or other professional advice or services, as may be required. The content and information in this book has been provided for educational and entertainment purposes only.

The content and information contained in this book has been compiled from sources deemed reliable, and it is accurate to the best of the Author's knowledge, information, and belief. However, the Author cannot guarantee its accuracy and validity and cannot be held liable for any errors and/or omissions. Further, changes are periodically made to this book as and when needed. Where appropriate and/or necessary, you must consult a professional (including but not limited to your doctor, attorney, financial advisor or such other professional advisor) before using any of the suggested remedies, techniques, or information in this book.

Upon using the contents and information contained in this book, you agree to hold harmless the Author from and against any damages, costs, and expenses, including any legal fees potentially resulting from the application of any of the information provided by this book. This disclaimer applies to any loss, damages or injury caused by the use and application, whether directly or indirectly, of any advice or information presented, whether for breach of contract, tort, negligence, personal injury, criminal intent, or under any other cause of action.

You agree to accept all risks of using the information presented in this book.

You agree that by continuing to read this book, where appropriate and/or necessary, you shall consult a professional (including but not limited to your doctor, attorney, or financial advisor or such other advisor as needed) before using any of the suggested remedies, techniques, or information in this book.

Table of Contents

Introduction 1

Chapter 1: What You Need to Know About Candles 3

    History of Candles 3

    Types of Candles 4

Chapter 2: Candle-Making Basic Supplies 7

    Wax 7

    Candle Wick and Stabilizer 9

    Candle Coloring Agents 11

    Candle Wax Additives 13

    Other Tools 14

Chapter 3: Candle-Making 101 17

    Step 1: Gather Supplies 17

    Step 2: Prepare the Wax 18

    Step 3: Prepare the Double Boiler 21

    Step 4: Measuring and Melting the Wax 21

    Step 5: Prepare the Molds 22

    Step 6: Add Color And/Or Fragrance 23

    Step 7: Allow the Wax to Cool 25

    Step 8: Pouring the Wax 26

    Step 9: Cool and Top Off 27

    Extra Steps for tea lights 28

Chapter 4: Advanced Candle Recipes 31
    Cuban Tobacco Container Candle 31
    Lemon Crème Candle 32
    Simple Wooden Wick Candle 33
    Autumn Potpourri Candle 34
    Bacon Candle Recipe 36
    Citronella Soy Wax Candle 37
    Triple Layer Candle Jar 38
    Ice Pillar Candle 40
    Coffee Cup Candles 41

Chapter 5: Troubleshooting 43
    Candle-Making Techniques 43
    Candle Storage Tips 47

Chapter 6: Resources and Supplies 49
    Wax 49
    Hardening Additives 49
    Coloring 50
    Scents 50
    Wicking 50
    Molds 50
    Should You Buy Wholesale or Retail? 51

Conclusion 53

Introduction

There's nothing more relaxing than going home and lighting a scented candle as you soak in your bath. Candles are versatile- they make you feel relaxed and can provide additional illumination in your home.

While you can easily buy candles at your favorite home improvement store, grocery store, or online store, wouldn't it be better if you could make one yourself? Making your own candles can be a fun activity. You can let your creativity run wild and create the kind of candles you like. Once you get the hang of making simple candles, you can create ones with various styles and designs.

Aside from sparking your creativity, one of the most important benefits when it comes to making your own candles is that you know exactly what goes into them. Some candles contain ingredients that are harmful to the body. Studies show that candles made from paraffin wax produce toluene – a highly toxic benzene also found in diesel fuels – when burned. Such candles may also release other chemicals when burned such as acetone, carbon disulfide, trichloroethene, chlorobenzene, styrene, xylene, and others. These compounds are found in products like paint, varnish, and stain remover. Moreover, some commercial candles use wicks that are laden with heavy metals like lead and a few hours of burning them can result in airborne heavy metals that you can breathe into your system.

If you make your own candles, you know which ingredients to include and which ones to omit. You can choose which scents to use or whether to opt for environmentally friendly beeswax over paraffin.

Making your own candles is not as difficult as you may think. Let this book serve as your ultimate guide.

Chapter 1
What You Need to Know About Candles

A simple way to illuminate your home is with candles, but there's more to them than that. This chapter will discuss what you need to know about candles.

History of Candles

Candles have been around to illuminate dwellings for more than 5,000 years. Although the first written texts about candles were in ancient Egyptian papyrus documents, little is known about the humble beginnings of candle-making. The Egyptians used torches made from reed and soaked them in melted animal fat, but they weren't true candles because they lacked wicks. The ancient Romans developed the technique further by dipping rolled papyrus in beeswax or tallow.

However, it wasn't only the Egyptians and Romans who developed wicked candles using waxes obtained from animals and plants. The ancient Chinese created candles using paper tubes rolled and dipped in wax from insects. The ancient Japanese made candles from wax sourced from tree nuts.

It was during the Middle Ages that candle-making became a cottage industry. The candles were made from animal fat called tallow. Beeswax was widely used and preferred as it produced a clean flame and emitted a pleasant smell compared to the acrid odor of animal tallow. It was during the 13th century that candle-making became a guild craft in France and England.

The candle industry grew even further when whaling became a big industry in the 18th century and provided a huge supply of spermaceti, or wax obtained from sperm whale oil. Just like beeswax, spermaceti does not produce any pungent odor when burned and burns brighter than other wax candles. It was harder than beeswax or tallow, thus the first standard candles were manufactured from spermaceti wax.

Most of the developments in candle-making occurred during the 19th century. This is when synthetic waxes were invented to create cheaper candles that sustained the demands of many households. Various materials were invented from stearin wax to paraffin wax. Moreover, machines were invented to create mass-produced candles that were affordable for the masses.

Types of Candles

If you're planning to make candles, it's crucial that you familiarize yourself with the various candles that are available on the market. Below is a list of candles that you can make:

- **Pillar candles:** self-standing and solid. They are typically cylindrical, but can take on different shapes including square, hexagonal, rectangular, and others. Pillar candles provide great accent to homes. When using them, make sure they are mounted on heat-resistant bases to collect the hot molten wax.

- **Floating candles:** have a stable profile and are designed to float on water. They vary in styles and designs.

What You Need to Know About Candles

- **Votive candles:** usually 2 1/2-inches in height and take on either the cylindrical or square design. They are burned in small, heat-resistant containers to collect the liquefied wax.

- **Taper candles:** called dinner candles, taper candles are usually 1 inch in diameter. They need to be securely set in the candle holder to catch melted wax. This type of candle burns faster than others.

- **Container candles:** called filled candles, the wax is placed in a heat-resistant or non-flammable container. They are popular gift items because they come in different containers.

- **Tea light candles:** usually 1 ½ inches in diameter. They are placed in a ¾-inch cylindrical metal container. These candles are used in food warmers and they don't last very long.

- **Gel candles:** one variation of container candle. It is made from a gelled mineral oil or synthetic hydrocarbon. It has a transparent and rubbery characteristic and can take on the shapes of its containers. The gel is soft, so it cannot support its own shape, thus it needs to be in a container.

- **Specialty candles:** come in a wide variety of shapes and sizes. They are molded or sculpted by hands to take on different designs and are mostly used for their decorative flare.

- **Liquid candles:** not technically candles. They are more like oil lamps. A wick is inserted through a metal holder and immersed in an oil reservoir.

Chapter 2
Candle-Making Basic Supplies

Candle-making has been around for centuries and was considered a basic life skill for many of our ancestors. If you didn't know how to make candles, you lived in the dark – simple as that! Before there was electricity, candles were the only artificial light source that illuminated homes. They were used as early as 3,000 BC not only for lighting homes, but also for religious services and other things.

When technology became more advanced, candles were no longer needed as an artificial light source. Today, making candles is an art that has survived the test of time and is still popular among people who love crafting. Candles available on the market today include pillar candles, votive candles, and container candles. It is important to take note that different candles require different ingredients.

For instance, upright pillar candles are made from hard wax as they are free-standing. Votive candles are small and they're placed in a container. If this is your first time making candles, this information will be crucial. This chapter is dedicated to educating you on the basic supplies involved in candle-making.

Wax

The most integral part of making candles is the wax. There are various waxes that you can use. It's important to take note that some waxes have different melting points, prices, and burning times, among other characteristics. Below are the waxes used in candle making:

- **Paraffin candle wax:** The least expensive type, paraffin wax is made from crude oil. It produces smoke and soot when it burns. It melts quickly and can be easily scented and colored.

- **Beeswax:** Beeswax is a natural byproduct of honey-making. It has a sweet fragrance and is more expensive than paraffin. You can get it in slabs or blocks. When heated, beeswax does not drip or produce smoke or soot. The caveat is that it does not retain color and scent well.

- **Natural palm wax:** Natural palm wax is derived from palm. It has long-lasting qualities and is smokeless. It's hard, which makes it good for pillar candles. However, it's more expensive than beeswax.

- **Soy wax:** Soy wax is made from soybeans and has a clean and slow-burning quality. It is a good alternative to the more expensive beeswax and natural palm wax.

- **Recycled wax:** As the name implies, recycled wax is what you get when you up cycle old candles. Making candles from recycled wax is a great way to reduce, reuse, and recycle old candles instead of throwing them out.

Candle Wick and Stabilizer

The wick is what you light up on your candle. Its size is important. As a general rule, smaller candles need smaller wicks and bigger candles need bigger wicks. It's crucial to know that different waxes go with different wicks. Attached to the wick is a stabilizer that holds the wick upright, especially if the wax has already been melted. Below is an in-depth discussion of what you need to know about candle wicks.

Wick Size

Getting the wick size right is important, otherwise your candle will not burn the way you expect it to. Below is a guide of wick sizes that you can use depending on the type of wax you use:

Diameter of Candle (mm)	Paraffin Candle Wax	Natural Candle Wax
Tea lights	Pre-waxed tea light wicks	Pre-waxed tea light wicks
25-50	LX10	ECO1
50-65	LX12	ECO4
65-76	LX16	ECO6
75-90	LX20	ECO10
90-100	LX26	ECO14

On the other hand, if you over wick, the candle can burn through the wax like butter and it'll be gone as soon as you light it up. You can extend the life of your candle by selecting the right wick size.

If, however, your candle is larger or wider, you might need to use multiple wicks to use up the wax more effectively.

Wick Types

There are different wick types you can use for different candles. Each type of wick has its own advantages and disadvantages. Below is a discussion of the various wicks you can use:

- **LX wick:** This type of wick is thin and flat. It curls into the flame thereby creating a self-trimming effect. This type of wick is designed for candles with a diameter of up to 55mm. It is suitable for votives or candles in small containers.

- **ECO wick:** This type of wick is made from flat cotton that is braided with thin paper threads, giving it a rigid structure. It does not come with a core, yet it can still support its own weight. It is an excellent choice for natural wax candles and it is great for pillars and container candles.

- **Pre-waxed wicks:** Pre-waxed wicks come in all sorts and sizes. They are already cut and attached to a stabilizer. This type of wick is great for shallow candles because you don't have to support the wick while the wax hardens. It is a great option for making tea lights and votives as well as molded candles.

- **Wooden wicks:** Wooden wicks are made from thin pieces of wood. They are about an inch wide and come in different lengths. You can use them in all waxes. Using a wooden wick is easier because it is more stable than ordinary cotton wicks.

Candle Coloring Agents

Coloring your candle can enhance its overall appeal. While most candle-making enthusiasts will tell you that only candles made from paraffin wax can be colored, other candles made from natural wax can too. If you are going to make candles at home, it's important to know what coloring agents to use. You cannot just use any dye available to color your candles.

Below are the dyes you can use to color your candles and how to achieve the right hue using the right amount of dye:

- **Liquid dye:** Liquid dye can be anything, but most people use food-grade dye because it's safe. The amount of liquid dye that you will need largely depends on how much wax you use. The more wax you use, the more dye you need to create an obvious tint. This means that the darker the color you want, the more dye you will need. Most people prefer to use liquid dye because it is easy to adjust the color. When adding liquid dye, start by using a small amount and stirring as you go. Continuously check the color until you are satisfied. Lastly, when adding liquid dye, do not add more than 20mL per kilogram of wax as too much dye can clog the wick.

- **Dye blocks or chips:** Another way to color your candle is to use dye block or chips. Made from vegetable-based wax that has a pre-measured amount of dye, dye blocks or chips can be directly added to melted wax. They produce duller color when compared to liquid dye. Add one chip for every 500 grams of wax. If you want a deeper color, add more as you go. However, avoid adding more than 8 chips per 500 grams of wax because it can clog the wick and affect the burning of the candle.

- **Dye flakes:** Used in making larger batches of candles, dye flakes can help you achieve a stronger depth of color. They are resistant to fading as they are highly concentrated. You only need a small amount of dye to achieve the desired color. They dissolve best when added to wax at 80^0C. Once you have heated the wax to the desired temperature, stir in the dye flakes and make sure that there are no undissolved flakes on the candle.

- **Broken crayons:** You can experiment with broken crayons to color your candles. The best thing about broken crayons is that they are extremely cheap and they come in different hues. However, since crayons have some impurities, they might cause the candle to burn unevenly or sputter.

Candle Scents

You can opt to make candles without scent but adding oils can turn a boring pillar candle into a luxurious one. As the wax begins to melt, it vaporizes the oil thereby producing a lovely aroma that will surely relax your body. There are various fragrances you can use. Below is a description of these scents:

- **Synthetic fragrance oils:** As the name implies, synthetic fragrance oils are fragrances that are made by mixing different compounds. As they are not natural, they can be inexpensive, thus making them great for those who want to make candles in large batches. However, some literature reports that synthetic fragrance oils can cause headaches and other reactions.

- **Essential oils:** A more natural way to make your candles fragrant, essential oils are derived from plants through the process of distillation. Although expensive, they have many potential benefits and are often used in aromatherapy.

When adding scents to your candles, it's crucial to only add a small amount so that the candle does not have an overpowering fragrance.

Candle Wax Additives

Candle wax additives are used to improve the quality of your candles. They can increase the firmness of the wax or soften it. Using additives gives you more control over your candles. Below are candle additives that you can use:

- **Palm TP stearic:** This compound can increase the firmness of your wax. It prevents the candle from losing its shape, especially in warmer weather.

- **Petrolatum:** Petrolatum is used to soften hard wax.

- **Stearic acid:** This is used to increase the whiteness of the wax. It makes it more opaque and helps hold free-standing candles such as tapered and pillar candles during the warmer seasons.

Other Tools

Aside from the basic ingredients, there are tools involved in making your own candles. This section will be dedicated to discussing the tools that you need to get started with candle-making.

Candle Molds

Candle molds are very important. Whether you make pillar candles, votives, or even container candles, you need a mold so that your candle can take shape. There are three basic categories of molds that you need to know about.

- **Metal molds:** Molds made from metal are common. They are often the mold of choice for pillar candles. What makes metal molds popular is their rigidity. They don't require additional support to hold the candle in place as it hardens.

- **Plastic molds:** Plastic molds are the cheapest and most often recommended to candle-making neophytes. They come in different shapes and sizes, so you can make wonderfully-shaped candles easily. Plastic molds are not the best when it comes to quality. Over time, they produce a scuffed or mottled appearance on the surface of the candle as they scratch and melt easily, especially when subjected to high heat. Moreover, they're not great for making scented candles as the oils can eat up the plastic and eventually ruin the mold.

- **Silicone molds:** Silicone molds are popular among people who want to make designs. They're versatile and flexible, thus they can make creative candle shapes. Moreover, they're easy to work with. Once the wax has hardened, just stretch the silicone and the candle pops out.

Candle Containers

If you want to make soft candles, then using a container is your best option. Candle containers come in different sizes and materials. The most common ones include glass and metal so choose one that meets your preferences.

Double Boiler

Melting your wax can be tricky. Make sure you don't melt it directly over the heat source as it will reach its flash point and burn or –worse – explode. Instead, melt your wax using a double boiler. You can get one to be used solely for melting wax. If you can't afford a double boiler, you can improvise by putting a metal bowl that you no longer use on top of a pan with boiling water.

Thermometer

While a thermometer is an optional tool when making candles, it's a good idea, especially if you need to precisely measure the temperature of the molten wax. This is especially true when adding coloring and scents that may require a certain temperature to work properly.

Others

Other items that you need are grease-proof parchment paper and a bamboo stick. The parchment paper is necessary to protect your work surface, especially if you don't have a dedicated station for making candles. The parchment paper will collect the melted wax so that you can easily remove it once it dries up.

The bamboo stick is used to provide support to the wick. If you don't have a bamboo stick, you can improvise by using a pen or pencil. You need a mold release spray so that you can easily remove the final product, especially if you are using a metal or plastic mold.

Chapter 3
Candle-Making 101

Candles come in a variety of styles, colors, and scents. Pillar candles, votive candles, tea lights, and container candles are all made following the same principles.

Step 1: Gather Supplies

Make sure you observe safety precautions as you will be handling hot wax most of the time.

Basic Ingredients	Basic Equipment
Wax	Double boiler
Wicks	Mold and mold sealer
Dyes	Thermometer
Scents	Kitchen food scale
	Wick holder

Step 2: Prepare the Wax

How much wax you need depends on the size and type of candle you want to make and the type of wax you're going to use. Remember that not all wax will yield the same volume of liquid wax once melted. Below is a simple guide to wax quantities:

- A pound block of paraffin wax can produce 20 liquid ounces of melted wax.

- A pound block of soy wax can yield 18 liquid ounces of melted wax.

- A pound of beeswax is equivalent to 16 liquid ounces of melted wax.

Determining how much wax you need requires trial and error. Factors like the temperature of the wax once poured and the temperature of the mold affect how much you should use. There are online calculators that you can try, but in my experience, calculating the amount of wax you need manually works best.

To do this, please refer to the steps below:

1. Weigh the empty container or candle mold and take note of its weight.

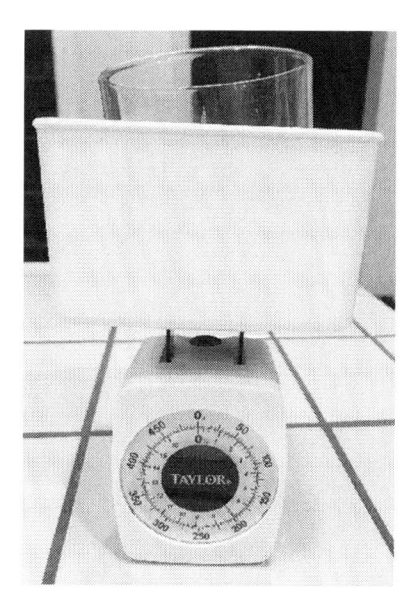

2. Fill the candle container with water and weigh it to get the total weight.

3. Subtract the weight of the empty container from the weight of the container with water to arrive at the amount of melted wax needed for one container.

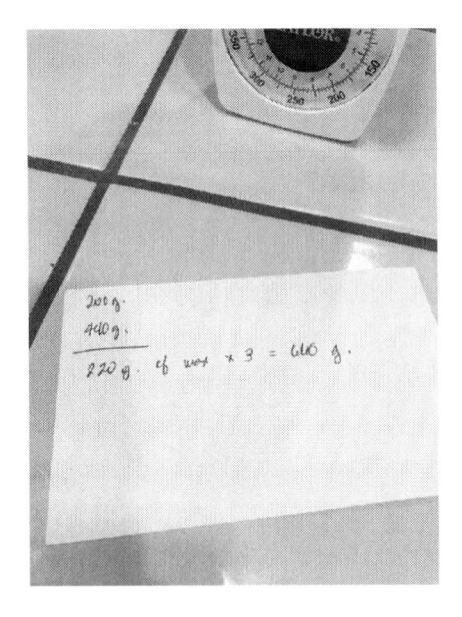

For example, I used a total of 220 grams of soy wax multiplied by three containers, so I needed to melt a total of 660 grams of wax. In my Jasmine Candle, I used the recipe below.

Simple Jasmine Candle Ingredients:

- 660 grams of soy wax
- 3 wicks
- 3 glass containers
- Jasmine essential oil

Step 3: Prepare the Double Boiler

The safest way to melt wax is to use a double boiler. If you don't have one, you can use two pans (see picture). If you are improvising, make sure that the first pan that contains hot water does not spill into the pot where the wax is, otherwise it will affect the final product. Place 2 inches of water in the first pot. The water will generate heat to melt the wax in the second pot.

Step 4: Measuring and Melting the Wax

When melting wax, safety is your number one priority. Never leave melting wax unattended. Constantly stir the wax while it is melting. How long you need to melt the wax depends on the type of wax you use and the temperature it needs to melt. Melted wax should look clear. The temperature of melted wax will be between 160 and 170 degrees Fahrenheit. If the temperature rises, take the pan off the stove.

Step 5: Prepare the Molds

If you're making tea lights, votives, or small pillar candles, then you need to put wick pins in the mold to ensure that the wick stays in place. Insert a straight wick in the wick pin and place it in the center of the mold before spraying with a mold release spray. For tea lights, the literature says the best wick size is 1" in length and 15x3.8mm in size. For other types of candles, you can use a longer wick depending on the length of the container. Set the wick in place and check the molds to ensure that the wick pins are properly centered during and after pouring the wax.

I use 16-ounce votive glasses. If you do not have a wick pin, use two pens to center the wick. To prepare the wick, dip the end in the melted wax and place it in the middle of your mold. With two pens or wick pins, hold the wick in place as it hardens and sticks to the bottom of the glass.

Step 6: Add Color And/Or Fragrance

Adding color and scent can improve your candle's quality. This is great if you're planning to give them away to your friends as gifts or sell them in the future. Scented candles also have benefits including relaxation, focus, and extra energy. For instance, a lavender-scented candle can make you relax or sleep better and a coffee-scented candle can boost your energy.

You can add either or both once the wax has fully melted. It is crucial that you use colors that are made for candles because the presence of impurities can make the candle burn unevenly.

Adding fragrance can be tricky—too much can affect the quality of the candle burn. While most references call for an ounce of fragrance per pound of wax, you can modify that depending on the strength you want. For my recipes, this is how I determined how much essential oil to use: (The right side of the equation is the constant. So, if you have a different weight for your wax, just plug it in the left side. X is what we are looking for- the amount of essential oil we need in the recipe.)

1. 660 grams of soy wax : *X mL of essential oil* = 450 grams (or 1lb of wax) : 30mL of essential oil (or 1 oz of oil)

2. 660 grams x 30mL = 450 grams **X**

3.
$$\frac{19{,}800 \text{g/mL} = 450 \text{ grams X}}{450 \text{ grams}}$$

4. **44mL = X**

HINT: Add your essential oil and coloring when your wax is between 130 and 140 degrees Fahrenheit. This range will not negatively affect the aroma or destroy the integrity of the aromatic compounds in your selected scent.

Step 7: Allow the Wax to Cool

It's important to allow the wax to cool before pouring it into molds. Knowing which temperature to pour the wax can determine the look and characteristic of the finished candle. Improper pouring temperature can result in the wax pulling away from the sides of the container. When cooling the wax, there are general guidelines to follow depending on the type of candle you're making:

- Container candles poured at 190°F.

- Votive candles poured at 190°F.

- Tea light candles poured at 130°F.

- Pillar candles poured between 175⁰F and 180⁰F.

Step 8: Pouring the Wax

Pouring the wax into molds is part science and part art. Handle melted wax carefully to avoid burns. Ladle the wax into a pour pot carefully. It's necessary to use a pour pot because it's designed so that you can effectively pour the wax into the narrow openings of your candle containers. It prevents the melted wax from spilling onto your work surface. Moreover, you can pour the candle in one go so it can cool evenly. Pour the melted wax into the glass candle holder slowly to avoid dislodging the wick pins placed in the middle earlier. Wax may still spill out of your pan while pouring. Don't worry, you can scrape it up once it cools and save it for future projects.

Step 9: Cool and Top Off

The cooling wax will sink and form a concave top. It's important to do another pour once the candles have cooled so you can create the tapered look at the tip.

Once the second layer of wax has cooled, cut off the excess wick. You should trim the candle wicks to 1/8". This will keep the flame nice and tidy and prevent the production of too much smoke. To do this, measure up from the base of the candle and cut.

You can begin using your scented candle immediately. Mine gave off a sweet-smelling aroma and lasted longer than name brand candles!

Extra Steps for tea lights

Removing the Finished Candles

Removing candles from the mold can be tricky. Make sure to let your wax harden completely before removing them to avoid scarring and tearing the wax from the surface of the candle. Using the mold release spray makes it easier to remove the candle from the mold. Gently tap the bottom of the mold and tug on the wick pin to loosen the candle from the mold.

If this doesn't work, submerge the hardened wax mold in hot water for a few seconds. You can warm the outside of the mold using a hair dryer if hot water is not available. This will soften the candle so that it will easily slide off the mold.

Placing the Wick

Once you remove the candle from the mold, turn it upside down and press the pin firmly against the tabletop to create a small hole where the wick can be inserted. Tug the wick from the top and secure it firmly in place. Make sure that the wick is at least ¼" before lighting. Enjoy!

Chapter 4
Advanced Candle Recipes

Cuban Tobacco Container Candle

Materials:

- Candle wax
- 8-ounce candle jar
- Cuban tobacco fragrance oil
- Wick tape
- Candle wick

Instructions:

5. Secure the wick at the bottom of the jar using the wick tape. This ensures that the wick will not move around once the hot wax is poured.
6. Prepare the wax by measuring double the amount of wax flakes into the jar. For instance, if the jar can hold a cup of dry wax flakes, you need two cups to fill a container.
7. Use a microwave-safe cup and melt the wax until smooth.
8. Remove from the heat and allow to cool for 5 minutes.
9. Stir in the fragrance oil. Stir for a minute.
10. Pour the scented wax into the jar.
11. Center the wick and stabilize it while it cools using a wooden skewer, popsicle stick, or whatever you have at home.
12. Allow the candle to cool completely.

Lemon Crème Candle

Materials:

- Soy wax
- Wick
- Lemon fragrance oil
- Candle container
- Hot glue gun

Instructions:

1. Secure the wick by placing a small amount of hot glue on the metal tab. Place the metal tab at the bottom of the candle container and press firmly in place. Set aside.
2. Prepare the wax by measuring double the amount of wax flakes into the jar. For instance, if the jar can hold a cup of dry wax flakes, you need two cups to fill a container.
3. Use a microwave-safe cup and melt the wax until smooth.
4. Remove from the heat and allow to cool for 5 minutes.
5. Add 1 ounce of fragrance oil per pound of wax used.
6. Carefully pour the scented wax into the container and make sure the wick is still in place.
7. Stabilize the wick by putting skewers or popsicles in between.
8. Allow to harden completely before trimming the wick.

Simple Wooden Wick Candle

Materials:

- 3 ½ cups candle wax
- 10 drops vanilla butter fragrance oil
- Mason jar(s)
- Wooden wick and metal clip(s)

Instructions:

1. In a double boiler, melt the wax and set aside to cool slightly.
2. Add fragrance and mix until well incorporated.
3. Dip the metal clip end of the wooden wick into the melted wax and secure it at the bottom in the center of the mason jar. Apply gentle pressure until the wax cools and sets the wooden wick in place.
4. Pour the melted wax into the mason jar and do not fill beyond the wooden wick.
5. Allow the wax to harden completely before burning.

Autumn Potpourri Candle

Materials:

- 10 lbs. beeswax
- Autumn woods fragrance oil
- 1 oz. yellow liquid candle dye
- 1 oz. red liquid candle dye
- 1 oz. orange candle dye
- 8 oz. clear candle jar
- Wicks
- Tiny leaf molds

Instructions:

1. Make the wax leaves first. Use a double boiler and melt 30 grams of wax. Use a toothpick and add a small amount of yellow dye. Stir well and allow the temperature to drop before adding 3 drops of fragrance oil. Pour into the leaf molds and allow to harden for several hours. Take them out of the mold and set aside.
2. Do the same steps for the red and orange dye.
3. Once all leaves have hardened, proceed to making the candle.
4. Place the wick at the center of the container.

5. Melt the remaining wax in a double boiler and allow to cool for 5 to 8 minutes or until the temperature reads 175°F.

6. Place the hardened wax leaves into the candle container. Be careful not to dislodge the wick.

7. Pour over the wax and allow to harden for a few hours before lighting.

Bacon Candle Recipe

Materials:

- 10 lbs. beeswax
- Bacon fragrance oil
- 1 oz. brown liquid candle dye
- 1 oz. red liquid candle dye
- Candle wicks
- Candle container
- Hot glue gun

Instructions:

1. Use hot glue to set the wick at the bottom in the center of the candle container. Set aside.
2. Melt the wax to 190°F in a double boiler. Turn off heat and add in the two colorings. Mix until the mixture becomes homogenous.
3. Allow to cool to 180°F before adding in 3 drops of fragrance oil. Let it cool further to 175°F before pouring into the candle container.
4. Carefully pour into the candle container making sure the candle wick stays in place.
5. Stabilize the wick by putting skewers or popsicles in between.
6. Allow the wax to harden completely before burning.

Citronella Soy Wax Candle

Materials:

- 1 lb. soy wax
- Citronella fragrance oil
- 1 oz. yellow liquid candle oil
- Hot glue gun
- Candle wicks

Instructions:

1. Place the wick at the bottom in the center of the candle container using a hot glue gun.
2. Warm the jar in the microwave oven for 15 seconds.
3. In a double boiler, heat 445 grams of soy wax until the temperature reaches 190°F.
4. Allow to cool to 180°F before adding the citronella fragrance oil.
5. Carefully pour into the candle container making sure that the wick stays in place.
6. Stabilize the wick by putting skewers or popsicles in between.
7. Allow the wax to harden completely before burning.

Triple Layer Candle Jar

Materials:

- 1 slab of beeswax
- 1 oz. red liquid candle dye
- 1 oz. blue liquid candle dye
- Candle wicks
- Red apple fragrance oil
- Blueberry fragrance oil
- French vanilla fragrance oil

Instructions:

1. Place the wick at the bottom in the center of the candle container using a hot glue gun. Set aside.

2. In a double boiler, melt 1/3 pound of beeswax and add 2 drops of blue dye until dissolved. Add 1 tablespoon blueberry fragrance oil. Once the wax reads 150^0F on the thermometer, pour into the candle container and allow to harden for a few hours.

3. Do the same thing to the rest of the colors. For the red color, melt 1/3 pound of beeswax and add the red dye until melted. Add a tablespoon of apple fragrance oil. Once the wax reads 150^0F on the thermometer, pour into the candle container

over the hardened blue wax and allow to harden for a few hours.

4. For the white color, use natural beeswax and do not add any color. Melt it and add in the vanilla fragrance oil. Once the wax reads 150^0F on the thermometer, pour into the candle container over the hardened blue and red wax. Allow to harden for a few hours and you are done.

Ice Pillar Candle

Materials:

- 10 lbs. pillar wax
- Lavender essential oil
- 1 oz. purple liquid candle dye
- Wicks
- Crushed ice

Instructions:

1. Work in an area where a sink is accessible.
2. Place the wick inside the mold (bottom center) using a hot glue gun. Set aside.
3. In a double boiler, melt the wax to 195°F and add purple liquid candle dye.
4. Allow the temperature to drop to 180°F before adding 1 ounce of essential oil.
5. Fill your mold with crushed ice and pour the wax over the ice.
6. Allow the wax to cool and the ice to melt completely.
7. Once the ice has melted pour out from the mold.
8. Gently remove the candle from the mold. If it is hard to remove the candle from the mold, submerge it in warm water for a few seconds.
9. Trim the wick and allow to dry before lighting.

Coffee Cup Candles

Materials:

- 1 16-ounce mug
- 1 lb. wax
- Root beer float fragrance oil
- Wick
- Whole coffee beans, roasted

Instructions:

1. Place the candle wick in the center of the mug. Use hot glue to secure the wick in place. Set aside.
2. In a double boiler, melt the wax up to 190°F.
3. Add a few drops of fragrance oil and allow the temperature to drop to 175°F.
4. Place coffee beans inside the container. Do this carefully to avoid dislodging the wick.
5. Pour the melted wax carefully into the container.
6. Allow to harden for a few hours before lighting.

Chapter 5
Troubleshooting

Candle-making is not easy and comes with challenges. You will experience problems such as candles not lighting well or producing too much smoke, among others. These problems can be frustrating, and you might want to stop making candles altogether. However, encountering these problems is normal and there are some things you can do to rectify them so that you can create candles like an artisan. Let this chapter serve as your guide to avoid or correct problems as you make your candles.

Candle-Making Techniques

There are certain techniques involved in candle-making that you need to learn by heart. Below are the best practices to follow when making candles.

Keeping Wicks Centered

Keeping the wicks centered can be tricky, but depending on the type of candles you make, there are several techniques you can use. If you are making votive candles, you can use a wick pin to ensure that the wick is properly placed in the center. If you are making container candles, you can secure the wick on top of the container with a securing bar. If you don't have a securing bar, you can use anything heavy to prop the wick on top of the mold. For example, you can use two sticks or books propped side by side to secure the wick in place while it hardens.

Ideal Temperature of Wax

Wax is poured between 120°F to 140°F. Pillar candles made from paraffin wax turn out better when poured at 180°F. Container candles are best poured between 170°F and 180°F. It is important to preheat your mold or container before pouring the hot wax, because it will crack when it comes into contact with a cold surface.

Preventing Air Bubbles in Candles

The presence of air bubbles or pockets will not only make your candles look unsightly, but it also affects the quality of their burn. Large air pockets will result in the flame constantly sputtering. To prevent air bubbles, heat the container or mold prior to pouring wax. While the wax is still hot, tap the mold on a hard surface to help release the bubbles.

Problems will occur when working with hot wax. To make it easier for you to resolve specific issues, here's a table with common problems and their solutions:

How To Make Candles

Issues	Reasons for Such Issue	Resolution
Small flame or flame drowns out	Wick is too small	Use a longer wick or try a different type of wick
	Wax is too hard	Use a softer wax or reduce the wax hardening used
Candle produces too much soot	Wick size may be too large	Use a smaller type of wick or try another type of wick
	Candle may be moist	Move the candles into an area that is not too drafty or dry it out completely
	Candle contains too many additives like dye or scent	Reduce the number of additives used in candles
Mushrooming of candle wick	Wick needs to be trimmed	Trim wick to ¼" or ½" before lighting
	Wick is too large or thick for the candle	Use a smaller wick or avoid using zinc wicks. Trimming wicks may help.
Candle flame too big	Wick is too long	Trim the wick to ½" to 1/2" prior to lighting them.
	Wick is too thick	Use a smaller wick or try other types of wicks
Candle color easily fades	Poor quality of dye used	Use only high-grade wax when making candles
	Low-grade wax used	Use high-grade dye for candles
	Too much exposure to sunlight	Always store candles in a dark place. Add UV inhibitor to prolong the color of the candle
Little scent throw	Wrong type of wax used	Use higher quality wax
	Adding fragrance oil too soon before pouring into the mold	Add scent just before pouring into the mold to minimize the effect of evaporation
	Poor quality of scent used	Use quality fragrance from reliable suppliers
	Too little scent oil used	Add more fragrance– but not too much!
Candle not burning evenly	The wick may be moist	Dry the candles thoroughly before lighting or move to area without draft
	Wick is not centered	The wick should be set at the center using a wick bar
Flames constantly sputtering	Air pockets are formed within the candle during the cooling process	Adjust the pouring temperature. The candle should not be too hot when poured. Tap the sides of the mold to remove air pockets.
	Water may have mixed into the wax	Prevent water from mixing into the wax during the candle-making process
Candle burns rapidly	Wax is too soft for the	Use hardened wax or use a smaller

Troubleshooting

Issues	Reasons for Such Issue	Resolution
	type of wick used	wick when making candles
	Air pockets are formed around the wick	Adjust the pouring temperature and tap the sides of the mold to remove large air pockets
Candle surface has a mottled look	Excessive amount of fragrance oil used	Reduce the amount of fragrance oil used. You can use additives to prevent the candle from mottling.
	Candle has cooled too quickly during the hardening process	Allow the candles to cool at a slower pace. To do this, wrap a towel around the mold during the cooling process. Preheat the mold prior to pouring the candle. Do not use too much mold release if applicable.
Candle does not stay lit	Wick is not primed	Use wicks that are coated with wax. These are called "primed" wicks.
	Wick is clogged	Avoid using dyes that may contain pigments that can clog the wick. You can clean the wax before lighting the wick.
Oil oozing from the candle	Used too much fragrance oil	Reduce the amount of oil used in making candles
	Wax is not created to retain large amounts of fragrance oil	Use wax that is designed to retain higher amount of fragrance oil. You can use additives to increase the retention of wax to fragrance oil.
Candle cracked during the cooling process	The candle cooled too abruptly	Allow the candle to cool in a warm place. Never place it in a refrigerator to harden.
Candle has large dye spots on the surface	Dye chips did not properly dissolve before pouring into molds.	When using dye chips, stir thoroughly to dissolve in the hot wax before pouring. You can use liquid dyes to make colored candles.
Candle color is fading	Candle is exposed to UV light for a long time	Store candles in a dark place and out of reach from direct sunlight or harsh UV light
Candle produces the tunneling effect or hard wax is left on the side of the container candle	Wick is too small	Use a larger wick or use a softer type of wax for even melting

Candle Storage Tips

To make your candles last, you must properly store them. Storing candles correctly can keep them looking new for a long time. This is especially true if you are making scented or colored candles.

- Keep candles in a cool, dark, and dry place. Avoid placing them in direct sunlight or harsh indoor lighting. Heat and sunlight can reduce the scent and cause the color of the candles to fade.

- Store tapered candles flat on a shelf or in a drawer because the presence of heat can cause the shape to warp.

- Use a damp soft or nylon cloth when cleaning the candles to remove dust and fingerprints.

- Never use a knife to remove wax drippings from pillar or votive candles as it can scratch or break the wax.

Chapter 6
Resources and Supplies

Some people are discouraged from taking on candle-making as a hobby because they think they don't have access to the supplies and ingredients they'll need. However, candle-making supplies are not hard to find- many people sell them online. Let this chapter serve as your guide on where to find the things you need to begin this rewarding hobby.

Wax

The most important ingredient in candle-making is wax. The best way to get wax is to buy directly from the supplier. If you plan to buy beeswax, get it from a local beekeeper. You can get paraffin from petroleum companies. You can also get wax from chemical suppliers, craft stores, or online. Ask for the minimum volume of wax that they'll sell. Some companies require buyers to purchase a minimum amount. Storing wax for long periods of time is not good, because it may degrade over time, especially if it's from natural sources (beeswax or soy wax). When buying wax, make sure it's pure, as the presence of contaminants will affect the quality of the burning candle.

Hardening Additives

Hardening additives are sold at local chemical companies, but they might require a minimum purchase amount of up to several pounds. You can find them online as well.

Coloring

There are various coloring options available to make your candles look exciting and attractive. While most experts swear by coloring chips or blocks, beginners should consider powder coloring as it is economical. You can find coloring agents at your local craft store or you can find a wider variety online.

Scents

There are many fragrance oils you can use to give your candles a pleasant aroma. The price of fragrance oils can range from $2 to $100 depending on the quality and type of scent you are planning to use. While synthetic fragrances are popular, you can also opt for essential oils as they provide more health benefits. You can buy scents from craft shops, but you will find better options online.

Wicking

You can buy wicks from your local hobby shop or many online shops. If you want to save money, buy wicks by the pound instead of by the yard. This will allow you to make a lot of candles to practice your skills.

Molds

Molds are easy to find at hobby stores. However, if you're looking for a specific design, then you have a better chance of finding it online. If you're new to this hobby, I recommend that you practice making container or pillar candles to familiarize yourself with the process. Once you're comfortable with candle-making and have learned a few techniques, only then should you experiment with different molds.

Should You Buy Wholesale or Retail?

It's tempting to buy wholesale. However, it's important to take note that you only need to buy enough ingredients to make the candles that you need. There is no point in buying 200 pounds of wax (even if it's on sale) if you're not going to make a lot of candles.

Conclusion

Making your own candles can be a rewarding hobby that you can eventually turn into a profit-making enterprise. You need to practice and develop your own techniques to make advanced candles. Aside from developing the right skills, it's important to invest in the right ingredients and equipment so that you can make artisan-quality candles. Let this book serve as your beginner's guide to creating candles.

If you've enjoyed reading this book, subscribe* to my mailing list for exclusive content and sneak peaks of my future books.

Go to the link below:

http://eepurl.com/dCTyG1

OR

Use the QR Code:

(*Must be 13 years or older to subscribe)

Printed in Great Britain
by Amazon